BREAKING OUT
OF THE COCOON

poems by

Lisa Rhodes-Ryabchich

Finishing Line Press
Georgetown, Kentucky

BREAKING OUT
OF THE COCOON

for my precious daughter
Kyla Jolie Ryabchich

ACKNOWLEDGMENTS

The following poems were published in their original or updated forms in the following
publications.

Ode to Reincarnation—*Burning House Press*
Mercy; The End; The Dream—*The Moon Magazine.*
Dearest Bastard—*Wrath Anthology by Pure Slush.*
The Cocoon—*Destigmatized: Voices for Change Anthology: Madness Muse Press*
Practice—*Medical Literary Messenger.*
Auntie Betty's Suicide 1969; Before You Committed Suicide; Memory; Divorce
        Papers; Suicide Planning; The Murder; Auntie Betty's Manifesto; The
        End; Elegy for Cousin Charles; Christmas; Details; The Wake; The Black
        Hole; Tragedy; Goodbye Cousin Charles and Auntie Betty—*Opening
        the Black Ovule Gate* Chapbook published by Finishing Line Press

I want to graciously thank my parents Joel and Rosemarie Rhodes for their belief in
my creative talents, Douglas Brown, Suzanne Cleary, Dan Masterson, Tom Lux, Kevin
Pilkington, Sarah Lawrence College, Cave Canem, Cornelia Street Cafe, Poets Corner
(where these poems were first performed), Shittu Fowora, Claudine Nash, Michael
Collins, Nicole Sealey, Denize Lauture, Bruce McEver, Martha's Vineyard Institute of
Creative Writing, Myronn Hardy, Cornelius Eady, Monica Youn, Evie Shockley, Michael
Affa Weaver, Gigi Silverman, Myra Goldberg, Joan Larkin, Rockland Poets, Dustin
Pickering, Jeffrey McDaniel, Nick Mazza, Greg Roman, Donald Fisher, Joan Silber,
Christopher Cipro, Dante Micheaux, Alexander Weinstein, Susan Guma, Jacqueline
Jones LaMon, Tyehimba Jess, Piermont Library, and countless others who have been
instrumental in providing support and encouragement for my poetry.

A special thanks to Finishing Line Press for helping bring this necessary work into the
world.

Publisher: Leah Huete de Maines
Editor: Christen Kincaid
Cover Art: Hyunju Min, "Color of Energy"
Author Photo: Glamour Shots
Cover Design: Lisa Rhodes-Ryabchich

Order online: www.finishinglinepress.com
                also available on amazon.com

Author inquiries and mail orders:
Finishing Line Press
P. O. Box 1626
Georgetown, Kentucky 40324
U. S. A.

Table of Contents

II.

I am alone here
in my own mind.
There is no map
and there is no road.
: Anne Sexton

SECTION ONE

BALANCE

To be emptied of grief
* * * * * * * * *
_ _ _ _ _ _ _ _ _
To escape the container
That held her freedom & soul
#################
To be free, to fly away like a bird—
Carefree
^^^^^^^^^^^^^^^^^^
To clean out all the cells that bound her
??????????????????????

AUNTIE BETTY'S SUICIDE 1969

After you committed murder
of your [son: husband] you climbed into
your white ceramic tub, turned on cold
water to the fill-line, slashed your thin
wrists to tissue-paper, and let your
10 pints of *Black/Portuguese* blood drip.

We all tried to patch up your unloved
veins with intellectual sutures,
then downed self-hate pills to stop the pain—
blocked the sore sun from shining in
our altered lives, and then my mother
masqueraded in green-tint sun-
glasses for most of her natural life.

DRESS REHEARSAL

Auntie Betty paid for her own elaborate wedding.
She practiced in a beautiful white taffeta dress
like a starburst—a ballerina from *Swan Lake*.

Her disinterested fiancé Charles never wanted
to go to dress rehearsals—
he never went to *any* dress rehearsals.

...

(1st sign he didn't love her).

...

She's a *dejected swan*, somehow less than an
angel to her fiancé Charles—

...

not a real *white swan*, pure, good and loving—
a fairy princess.

...

Now she is the *black swan of death* dressed in black icicles,
and he made her marriage to the grave.

WILL YOU MARRY ME

Auntie Betty asked her fiancé,
Charles, to marry her.
Where in the 1960's did any woman
have that kind of boldness?

Or, was it desperation to *fit in*—
to-be-seen with a handsome man—
to project the image of having made it.

Wedding pictures were snapped,
on the wedding day—her posing gorgeous,
in a long, white satin, illusive ball-gown
dress with a long train,

and a poufy, white, lace veil with white mesh
flowering around her pretty face.
Her smile and confidence lit up the church
when she sauntered down the aisle,

as her *mama's-boy* fiancé grinned,
clutching her kind hands as she arrived.
Was she just another sister, who would
continue, to nurture and mold him

into being a man?
Why had he robbed her of her chance
to find love? by preying on her weaknesses
like a *sycophant*—another species.

Something she didn't know was how to escape,
the clever bastard, who didn't know how-
to-be a man or a father or a good husband—
something he would never quite attain in his lifetime.

EMBOLISM

Auntie Betty had an embolism
when she was in her 30's.

Do you know how the embolism
manifests? —In the mind or in the soul?

No one remembered the details
of what she went through—

from hospitals or rooms,
apocalypse or civilizations—

how much pain she suffered—
or how she was able to get to a doctor,

or what medicine they put her on,
and how this affected her life—

her marital and career choices
and her mind and why.

Do you think death connects
inside the brain like a dendrite?

What did she think
about her own life expectancy?

What did her doctor warn her
not to do?

What were her chances
of having another embolism?

And in the brain do you excavate
your ancestral seeds of compassion?

What did this mean for her child?
There was a family history of strokes.

Did her husband know of her condition?
And what would it have prevented?

Do you not wonder
where the joy from the child lived?

What did her autopsy report say?
If another embolism

had clotted her arteries,
would the pain have caused her to panic—

to cause her a nervous breakdown
leading to more devastating consequences?

Do you not see that the honey bee stings
only once to, then die afterwards?

Was she always preparing for her own death—
by knowing she could have another embolism,

which might kill her unexpectedly—
in her sleep, in her thoughts, and in her mind?

BEFORE YOU COMMITTED SUICIDE

I remember you grabbing the black steel
pan off of the greasy white stove,
then waving it at my mother like a hammer
as you screamed, "Your husband made a pass at me!"

My mother just looked at you right in
your eye and sadly said, "No, No!" Six-year-old I
was there watching you in that cramped
Bronx kitchen. The three of us only inches

apart. I didn't flinch or run to my
mother to protect her or try to
grab the pan out of your hand. You accused
my father of something terrible,

and I can't imagine he would have
wanted you! You were confused and jealous—
a copycat. My mother was an RN,
then you became one too. My mother

married a handsome man, then you married
one too. Why did you try to become her?
Why did you want everything she had?
Once you told my mother,

"If you ever commit suicide,
I'll take your children for you."
What a monster mother you turned out to be.
I am not like you nor will I ever be.

MEMORY

Your boyfriend did something very
terrible to my sister. I
did not know this then. My mother
later told you that she was very
angry; I never knew this…Years
later my sister told her friend
about it: the reasons why she
never got married. I wondered
if this was true. She had no memory
when asked, only a church girl sits
on the couch, only some memory
exists after your death, and my
mother's silent indifference
and refusal to contact you then.
I understand anger; I understand shame.
A child's frightened eyes tiptoe
through darkness. I've tried to go back
there, walking through that apartment
as a child, on that day, and you're
still sitting on the radiator
with your boyfriend staring me away.
*It's dark. I don't know why he is
in our apartment; he shouldn't
be here.* Were you so insecure
about yourself that you needed
someone to watch you? Why did you
bring him there? Was this what your life
was reduced to after the breakup—
hanging out with your boyfriend?
You were much prettier than that.

MERCY

What if—
my mother had visited you
in your hour of distress and
confronted the child within you?—

The proud child that stood next to her,
after she graduated from high school,
as she posed hopeful with her blue cap
and gown on and tassel pulled to the left.

The child you played with at Christmas,
posing in front of your family's tree
with silver tinsel, and colored flashing
lights gleaming like miraculous stars.
Both of you friends together at age nine.

Would things have been different—if she had
shaken you from a depression
like a fallen leaf, spinning to its untimely death
in the autumn air—gracious like a ballet dancer
pirouetting—before suddenly landing flattened?

Would you have listened with an open heart
to her pleas for *mercy*—to forgive the feuding past
and what troubled you both, then opened a new page
of poetry to mend all the sharp words flung,
like knives tasting *amargo* on your tongues?

Could you have made homage to it?
—and taken a vow to go past it—
if she had said, "Sister, I forgive you?"

DIVORCE PAPERS

I remember the day you burned
                              your husband's clothes
                                 in the incinerator

after he walked out on you...
He told my dad that was it... if you ever did that again
                              he was through...

He was such a *Bastard* as he shoved
the divorce papers down your throat—under your door

when you were sleeping   after he got what he wanted:
your money & empathy   for his latent ways.

CHARLES JR TRYING TO BE LIKE JESUS

Benevolent, kind, loving, & forgiving?
Charles Jr. unforgiving & hating her...

"You don't love me!"
"You're a big monster!"

Charles Jr. seen as *Judas* opening
Hell's gates for his mother &

she blamed him for ruining her marriage,
but he still prayed everything would be all right.

"Where's Daddy?"
"When will Daddy be here?"

His mother furious &
hating & not feeling—

relieved & free to kill
which made her life hell—

which did not bring her joy—
who was made in the spitting image

of the man who never loved her &
she imagined Charles Jr. never loving her too,

being poisoned
by his father's disgust &

never being able to consummate
a good relationship with him.

His mother acting revengeful,
seeing Charles Jr. as an object of punishment

for his father's rejection of her—
seeing Charles Jr.'s life ruined because of the divorce;

fear of Charles Jr. becoming gay
after being abandoned by his father,

since his father wanted nothing to do with her,
he wouldn't continue to visit Charles Jr.

It would be unbearable to see him weekly
—the situation was unfixable & hopeless.

SUICIDE PLANNING

She milks her lone child. Did she kiss him goodnight
with red Morning Glory lipstick? Apply a rouge
color to his already *Santa Claus* rosy cheeks?

She loves her hunky husband—paying to send him
to finish his B.S. in Economics degree.
How much did she love him when contemplating their

son's death? Did she decide after a jealous flir-
tation in the kitchen, after sex was washed from
the dinner plate? Or did she plan his heavenly
breathtaking after two weeks of unrequited angst:

A divorce paper quickly jammed under her door
and her younger sister's husband's friendly visits
to console her, and the stigmata of *Black crazy single mom.*

PRACTICE

She was used to death and preparing the body
for the bereaved family,
carefully cleansing and positioning the limbs,
combing the hair until soft,
then arranging the furniture in the room,
and afterward

draping the expired body with a white sheet—
wrapping it like a *gift box*
inside a black zippered bag—
then releasing the paused curtains,
unveiling the sun setting over the empty body.

She must have prepped babies for the morgue too...
seen them die, their breaths extinguished like light,
evaporating into darkness—
gradually disappearing from the soft skull,
leaving the body barren—
yearning for forgiveness, for solace.

THE MURDER

[Inside his depraved mother's head] it's better
this way—she shows me her evil smile
as the Joker from *Batman*.

[Inside my cousin's head] he shows me tragedy—
          the confusing white, hospital-grade pillow imploding—
his mother's hands pushing down a plastic bag around his head
          forcefully as steel pincers.

[Inside my head] his little boy/man body was being
taken, until finally there was no struggle.

                    *

Why could he not fight her rage?
Why did he have no strength?

Did she drug him before?
Did she sing him soft lullabies as to a newborn?

                    *

Your father and his family went
to [your funeral]—
I can remember his frantic, depressed, handsome
figure passing through the black crowds of adults.

He later blocked you out like an aborted fetus.
He remarried and told no one about you.
Your birth was *lobotomized.*

                    *

When your prominent father died—I'm sorry,
there was no mention of your *name.*

AFTERWARD

What must it have felt like to commit murder?
—the murder of your son's soul now etched
into your brain like a *satanic star.*

You detached yourself like an overzealous
honeybee who, after stinging its prey,
suddenly dies immediately afterward.

Or was it your way of wanting to rob
your son of any revenge?—
by refusing to bear witness to his death.

His face was purpling, like a distorted eggplant,
growing stranger, with the stench of death
and the unbearableness of his own corpse.

DEAREST BASTARD

Dearest Bastard, you have finally done it this time!
Pushed me over the edge—
saw me standing there, wavering
unsure and unsettled, hair all a muss
and teeth unbrushed.
My breath is rancid with rage;
the garlic has caught my tummy on fire!
I'm the last dancer on this mad merry go round, and
I'm tired of being pushed around!
You've offered me the door, the cold, indiscreet
divorce—now here is the *coffin birth* you've wanted for
so long—you might as well have planned it yourself!
I've done everything to please you,
birthed your child, paid for your school—the wedding—the rings,
even invited your gruesome sisters for dinner, during the holidays.
Now I'm finished, listening to your weary, sad tale of *marital blues,* and
I'm done!
Go ahead you *cowardly Bastard,* give yourself a hearty pat on the back.

AUNTIE BETTY'S MANIFESTO

What was it like for me?
A Black woman in 1969
being served divorce papers—
the stigma? the shame?—
having an undiagnosed mental illness.

No treatment… just shunned—thrown away
like garbage—a cast-off?
Suicidal anyway.
Could *one* win? Could there have been
any hope? I remember

Francis Farmer—her life was ruined.
She was seen as a sad lady—
crazy and useless. Insulin jabbed
into her vein; she was left
emotionally vacant.

I remember my mother's sister Suzie—
her boyfriend kidnapped their daughter
because Suzie had a *nervous breakdown.*
Her daughter was never found.
I didn't want to lose my son.

Could one win?
No, No, I don't think so!
Men were not kind and forgiving.
My experience and what I knew of the world—
and what was taught to me by my father.

My mother was often beaten
by my father.
She almost died many times.
For mother: Black and blue,
I watched you struggle…

How you made it through, *God only knows.*

Who was there to stop him? No man
or brother, no neighbors—
I was just desperate to find love
from a handsome man.

I never saw any love in my father.
Born on his birthday—
I'm an outcast, somehow stigmatized by his blood,
his illness—his niceness towards *only me* and
not to my mother.
Oh God, how you have us all confused.

THE END

Why was I jealous…?

            Competitive?
            I was pretty.

To be driven by self-respect, tenacity, resilience…
Where was mine? I copied my sister; I wanted to be her.

She was my role model, my *surrogate* mother.
I was nice to my nieces; I really loved them.

Pushed over the edge… from a loveless relationship—
It happens. I was outraged. My paychecks paid his tuition.

Desperation made my self-esteem low…
            Illness can be so strong.

I was *Full* of self-hate… a desire to die. I was so confused.
I felt used—I didn't want a divorce.

Revengeful, I took my seed with me.
End the family, I told myself—total self-rejection. .

I felt *cast away* like a bad seed, rejected & dejected.
Feeling like a whore who was going to be screwed—

a *failure*, I was ashamed—embarrassed…
            I felt unloved, disillusioned by a lie

that I was ever in a *loving* relationship.

OUTCAST

What did they say your name was?
An *outcast*?
You don't fit in like us—
our father dotes on you
but not us.

You are the *star of heaven*—
the insufferable one, partying
together with Daddy
on his birthday—your birthday,
in a secret union, in silence, as a witness—
made to be an accomplice.

You were brainwashed
to be his secret conspirator.
Daddy's name was Joseph,
but he did not foster father Jesus.
He was like Joseph Stalin, a merciless dictator!
Nor were you the Virgin Mary—
the kind mother of baby Jesus.

You were made to endure,
but were secretly hated, and envied. Why
did you let your life become such a total hell?
What victimization did you not suffer?
What could we have done to undo your pain?

THE DREAM

My Auntie Betty came to me in a dream
dressed in an unsightly long black dress
reaching the ground,
with a black lace veil covering her despondent face.

She wore long black gloves, and black rosary
beads hung around her neck.
She was walking around Rockland Cemetery's
front lawn, asking for *forgiveness.*

I saw tears hiding
over a young girl's face.
She had not aged in death.

Why had I imagined that she would get *old?*
If I had gone insane—
how would I want to be remembered?
Querido Deus when does the suffering end?

ODE TO REINCARNATION

I wonder if Auntie Betty believed in reincarnation?
A friend's father once told me:

The dead are really still here.
You can't see them, but they are in the background.

I have come to believe this strange tale, and
I find the presence of the dead less distasteful.

Do the dead want to comfort the living?
I have witnessed strange things:

flashlights turning on suddenly in my apartment—
then music playing by itself, and

objects appearing when I most needed them,
in full view with ease of access.

Now, I feel warmth by ghostly presences
in my mind, and I am less lonely.

I recently imagined my Auntie mourning
her only son's death

in the afterlife and being present at my burial.
Is she a martyr of death?

Will she leave this pitying circle of tragedy
and move on without us looking back?

When will our scars become healed?
When will we all become *whole* again?

DEATH IMAGINATION

What must it have been like
to die in the tub with your arms and wrists cut
like Christ crucified on the cross?

Was it to feel just some ounce of pain—
to rid the numbness, or to feel empathy?

For to not know halfway through it—
if you will be somewhere in the next life…

Was my Auntie Bettie, a sort of Dr. Kevorkian, enabling
her son's soul to passage to a better life,
like freeing the enslaved child from its chains?

Because what is this life?—
when it chokes you around the heart,
and there are no more openings in the sky—
when the magicians have stopped making magic.

What must her thoughts have been?—
when planning her escape, after she committed murder.
Was murdering herself,
an act of *retribution,* before meeting Christ?

Would Christ have comforted her more,
seeing how she had suffered,
or was it her way of showing her family
how she was *tortured,*
in mind, body, and soul or just a cowardly act?

Should she have stayed to face the crime
and do penance on Earth?
Is there penance in the afterlife?

Do we reincarnate into another life form?
Will we have to pay for our sins of this life?
Can we ever get it *right*

after committing such a tragic act?

Are we at least like *Pinocchio* with friends
to guide us into being a better person?
Is natural death like walking on puffed clouds at night,
or onto the blues of sky matter, traipsing over
each lush hollow of stardust bringing you higher and higher
into transcendence—so peaceful and beautiful?

But what of suicide?
Those who want to commit suicide—
who have it well planned
and who have found peace with their dying—
have they reached an *epiphany* of joy?
And what of the experience—what will it be like?

Must it be quick for one to do this
or lose that rapturous ideology?
If one dies like this after committing murder,
have they gone *insane*?

Or just found the sanity to escape their assassins
on the way, by depriving them of the *joy* of killing them.
Or did good Jesus goad her and tell her:
"Come with me sister; life will be beautiful!
Come enter the *Kingdom of Heaven*—all will be forgiven."
And if Jesus did, would you have gone his way?

AUTOPSY REPORT

What did it find out about
her husband's *cold* indifference?

Did her husband ever suspect foul
play? Did the police ever think
he was a suspect in the case?

She left no note…
no tape-recording, no last video.

Were her fingerprints on the plastic
bag used to suffocate Charles Jr?

Did she have a schizophrenic break?
How would one know?

Did she hear *voices* in her head, ordering her
to kill her son and herself?
There was a history of mental illness.

But why would it happen now, after three years of
parenting, amidst all their fighting and separations?

Was she enraged by her husband's other lovers?
Did she receive threatening phone calls?—

to *end* her life and her son's life
from one of his lovers?

What were their fights about?
Bad sex, or no sex with him

never being at home—then coming home late,
with a lame excuse, and another lover's

perfume reeking on his body, or lipstick
protruding from his shirts?

Maybe that's why she burned his clothes?

Maybe they were about him not paying her
any attention or having quality time for baby Charles?

But another woman—
or man—this would hurt the most.

This would be death! The flames for *Satin*
to take spiritual possession.

She was a very jealous woman,
who only wanted a kind man

to love her with all her flaws—
not a male *sociopath* to live off her for her money.

She was his mark, and he was remorseless.
He became a nasty parasite that she couldn't exterminate.

And Charles was just getting ready to graduate.
He didn't need her anymore.

She's old news—a declawed tiger
ready for the zoo—for a circus show.

Was this the way he timed his arguments?
One per semester—right after final exams—

then makeup sex until the next tuition check?

He was a charlatan and she was his gypsy.
Only she had no more tricks to play.

He had erased all her mystery,
and the magician in her had exhausted all options.

Her legacy he selfishly destroyed.

LAST WISHES

Maybe there could have been one last miracle—
just one last chance to rethink everything over and over,

from rescuing small flowers to leaves of clover—
to remember you survived being a witness

to your mother's abuse—
the bedside hospital vigils, listening to her

labored breaths all Black and blue—
to remember you survived your childhood

living in a homeless shelter—
the leery men and drunken bums, their crazy vodka stench—

to remember you survived seven other sisters, sobrevivir!—
their wild dreams and inflated self-esteem.

Oh, how miraculous you were!—
to survive an embolism

and the prodding of your cerebrum for blood
clots like a tiny atlas—

to survive postpartum depression:
The baby doesn't look like me, you screamed silently—

to survive your mother's house of rats and roaches—
the nursery of daily filth, leftovers from yesterday's specials—

to survive your character assassination—that would have
been like becoming a fugitive running to evade injustice!

Too bad you couldn't have met a man
who had a kind heart of a giant!

Too bad your life was tangled like a thorn bush
strangling your soul.

If only there was a dating site for the *beautifully mad and single mothers.*

If only there was snow in the air…
If only, if only, if only…

AUNTIE BETTY'S RETRIBUTION PRAYER

Here in the afterlife, I can see all your faults—
your fears that you have meticulously

tried to hide. I watch you idling the edge
unaware. I in my death am strong now,

endowed with healing powers. Cowrie shells
adorn my eyes. I can warn

you of all tragedy bestowed upon you by your enemies.
I am the *eye of tragedy* that has retributed my sins.

You will not have to suffer on earth as I did.
You will have no more pain and agony.

You will be protected. I will be your seer
guiding you through the brambles and bones

to the *Kingdom of Heaven*, there on earth.
There shall be a meditative healing!

No night shall tear at your *Raggedy Ann heart*—
only the stars will glimmer stories of hope.

I WANT TO BE A SHAMAN

We are all shamans looking to heal the soul
of the deceased—forgive them for all their sins,
help them pay retribution to those they harmed.

We carry their tears, like a crucifix across the ocean's
floor—deep into hell, past the broken ribs of Christ,
past the gold teeth of Satin.

We sin—we slave for forgiveness!
Where did you say this life would take us?
To heaven—where is that?

What illusion gets us there?
Do the great ghosts dance us to sleep?
—to never be remembered again?

I want to believe you—
when you say *you're sorry.*

I want to trust you—
when you say *you're healed!*

I want to love you like I was a *good little girl.*

ELEGY FOR AUNTIE BETTY

You browned in the Bronx sun.
You died wrist slit open in a Harlem apartment.

You grew like an exotic wildflower.
You were a magnolia all sweetness and honey.

You were a child of God.
You were twilight emerging from Heaven,

after a downpour—after everything
seemed doomed to disaster.

You were sand breaking back
from high tide.

You were a flower box, a cardinal singing
joyfully in spring.

You were loved the day you were born—
a piece of hope that built more time

in a marriage that bled out.
You were a *fallen angel*—

a witch possessed, taken by demons
on a cot to the cemetery, one night

in a parade procession.
You were the alpha and the omega.

You became a black hole, doomed
to encounter lost souls.

You were pudding and pineapple,
mud and sticks, and stones.

You were dog hair and brambles—
thorns around Christ's head,

then a caterpillar, black and furry
creeping along an oak tree.

You were the jailer's keys on a *gold* chain.
You were the baby doll, angel-eyed

Christmas present to the world—
molasses and brown sugar, soft nougat

candy bar melted on the tongue—
the white fur choked by a Condor's neck,

a flapper singing lullabies for women's rights—
an actress without an audience,

who played the muse.
You were cinnamon toast and hot *ghee*

on a Sunday morning.
You were skinny, rust corduroy pants

and a plaid vest, poised for September *Vogue*.
You were the last teddy bear, won at the carnival,

by a random knife thrower who stabbed
the poor girl in the heart.

You were warm Ritz Crackers
deserving only the finest caviar.

You were the "SMILE" button
that performed random acts of kindness—

the wrinkle crème for the mentally infirmed
and severely deranged.

You were pancakes and hot honey
syrup on Easter Sunday,

and a teaspoon of virgin olive oil,
smooth and mellow.

You were a baby mushroom growing
wildly after a summer rainstorm.

You were a Sunday ride to the country—
all sassafras and spearmint leaves.

You were blueberries n' cream and whipped
sweet-potatoes at a house-warming picnic.

You were resilient, like a sunflower, growing
in an abandoned wishing well.

You were charisma, in chic sneakers, listening
to Mozart's *Symphony No. 40.*

You were lemon meringue pie with whipped
sweet cream at Chock Full O' Nuts Café.

You were a unicorn
who liked warm oatmeal

cookies and cold milk,
after watching a blockbuster movie.

You were blackberry wine
and a fresh bag of lemons

freshly squeezed
for summer lemonade.

You were the peppermint schnapps
at Christmas time—

with fake long lashes
and your long black fall.

Your portrait made the stereopticon look silly.

You were Sister Bertrille,
magical and mysterious—

like firecrackers
on the Fourth of July.

You were Indian summer,
all golden brown,

tanning gloriously
under a fiery red sunset.

*Then quiet like a pretty sailboat
during an orange glowing sunrise.*

You were a baby ivory plant,
climbing endlessly—

trying to thrive
amidst the pick of the male litter.

You were a life jacket touching the endless
sky—searching for *Nirvana.*

You were a toy girl-soldier, playing snow
croquet, who sang soprano in the church choir.

You were a Happy Birthday card,
sent by skywriting—

and a bouquet of yellow roses,
sent by TLC.

You were a knock-knock joke,
all-full-of surprises,

like warm red-flannel pajamas,
with yellow-print hearts.

You were freshly baked raisin bread,
served on a snowy day,

and smelled sweet, like vanilla
frosting on a Duncan donut.

You were a cherry Tootsie Roll
lollipop, soft and sweet inside—

and cheery on the outside, like a
glass of fine red wine.

You were a *Mercedes Benz 260 D,*
everywhere you went,

people wanted to know
more about you—

your endless passions,
your creative powers—

and listen to your idyllic voice,
strolling down the avenue.

You were the *Statue of Liberty*
on Staten Island,

who dreamed of ballet dancing
in *The Nutcracker Suite.*

You were a clairvoyant
who received an April fools telegram—

your first love letter signed
by a secret admirer at age five.

You were sweet dreams and wild imagination,
like confection sugar, poured

over a bar of Fairtrade,
dark, raspberry-filled chocolate.

You were a child's first set of fake nails
brought from the Five & Dime store,

and a bottle of romantic-red nail polish
poised when stressed for success.

You were root beer
and black licorice

on a Friday night,
at the local drive-in movie theatre.

You were that gooey soft cacao bean,
given to me by a tour guide

in Ocho Rios, Jamaica
during college winter break.

You were my green Conure parrot
that was given away by mistake.

You were gumdrops
and ginger trees and snow flowers,

and the heartbeat
of an unborn miracle baby.

You were baptized at the beach
with the tide racing in,

then driven back out
like a razzmatazz angel.

You were classical violins and French bread,
while walking along

Museum Row on Fifth Avenue,
in New York City.

You were cool winter breeze
and cobblestone sidewalks,

taking me gently
to private grammar school.

You were an old-fashioned milk bottle,
and the foamy layer

of pure cream
wafting off the top.

You were my white gloves
praying at my First Communion,

and the knobby knees of a First Grader
learning to play tennis.

You were a lemon-lime Starburst,
and a colorful array

of vintage soda caps
collected from the 1950's.

You were guacamole and chips,
served at a restaurant in *Seville, Spain*

and my first Spanish lesson,
Hace lo bien.

You were the Green Hornet
who wore mini skirts

and lived lavishly
in a phone booth.

You were the rare Liberty silver dollar
saved by your mother's

hobby of coin collecting
and given to me on my birthday.

You were the restless legs,
exhausted and happy,

wanting to stretch
and run a 20-mile marathon.

You were my private school uniforms:
Hush Puppy shoes—

pink or yellow cotton skirts in summer, a
red burgundy wool skirt in winter.

You were a pint of chocolate fudge
Glace ice cream

and pleasantly aromatic, like
a grove of wild pink orchids.

You were the cracks in the sidewalk
that I didn't want to step on,

hopscotching my way every day
down near Fifth Avenue.

You were a dancing dragonfly
buzzing overhead, like a prehistoric

dinosaur, ghosting quietly
at a summer writing seminar.

You were my first mood ring,
dazzling in yellow, turning pink to green,

light green to blue-green, blue then indigo,
darker blue to violet to burgundy light glowing.

You were my red carpet, perfectly
vacuumed and sun shadowed

that I guarded like a royal tomb,
watching for footprints of intruders.

You were sweet, like a slice of applesauce
raisin cake, and a Little Suzy homemaker,

watching Julia Child,
as you baked your first lasagna casserole.

You were a kindergarten finger-painting
in orange, on white glossy-paper,

framed in my museum-like mind,
for all-of-eternity.

You were a 10-foot Hoagie sandwich
and a cream-filled, chocolate Yankee Doodle cupcake

worth marching for two miles,
in summer day camp, in 1969.

You were my red Hula Hoop and a pencil box
with a coveted made-in-China eraser

that looked and smelled like
a square piece of fruity candy.

You were white ankle socks
and a big, pink Easter hat,

and my favorite light-blue, Saks Fifth Avenue
box pocketbook with a long gold chain.

You were pink wafer cookies,
and the *Mother Goose* storybook

read out loud to me
in kindergarten.

You were ocean foam and seaweed mixed
with sand, salt and brine, seashells and stars.

You were a classy Jackson Pollack painting,
Number 5, 1948,

showing off
at the Guggenheim Museum.

You were a raucous pair
of red and black

Pippi Longstocking leg warmers
dazzling like two licorice-peppermint sticks.

You were a Tic Tac Toe board.
I was the Tac,

and Leslie was the Tic,
and we won many games.

You were a bowl of thick spaghetti and red
sauce with fresh oregano and cilantro.

You were a holiday tin of Swedish butter
cookies, indescribably delicious and addictive.

You were the *star crèche nebulae*
formulating new dreams

to expand the universe
and raise our consciousness.

You were the southern, white clapboard house,
with black shutters

and an antique lion,
guarding the front gate.

You were the borrowed 1800's
pink waist dress, which I wore

to a friend's senior prom,
that got stolen by the dry-cleaning store.

You were like an Alaskan husky puppy,
walking in Central Park,

in summertime, and as ambitious
as a cross-country trekker.

You were as pretty and as talented
as Vivian Leigh,

and you could have been
a starring Hollywood actress.

You were majestic like the water fountain
at Lincoln Center in New York City,

attracting exotic people
from around the world.

You reminded me of Audrey Hepburn
in *Breakfast at Tiffany's*,

and I imagined you wearing long black leather
gloves and a leopard coat,

dangling your fake cigarette,
inside a black cigarette holder

as if in a pose for *Who's Who Magazine*.
You dreamed to visit Paris—

The Louvre, The Eiffel Tower,
Le Musée d' Orsay,

Chateaux de Versailles, Rive Droit,
The Paris Métro—

I visited there for you twice.
I told them *Merci Beaucoup!* for you.

You were a Sturbridge Farms assortment
of penny candies, caramel creams,

Chiclets gum, red licorice, *Good & Plenty*,
and a big, red, shiny candy apple.

You were a purple bar of lavender
victorian soap and a pan of fresh gingerbread.

You were a hot cauldron of vegetable soup
and a hunk of Italian bread

after walking ten New York City blocks
in freezing winter weather.

You were candlelight during a blackout
and comforting like a warm thick blanket

to cuddle up next to
when the cold ache got into your bones.

You were kind like the sweet, mini apple
pie I devoured at a Girl Scouts festival

where I dressed as a Pakistani,
with my long sari wrap-around skirt.

You were the Cat's Cradle string game
Leslie and I played endlessly,

unsolving all its intricacies
and creating new designs.

You were a red box of Valentine's Hearts
saying *I love you*

in ten different languages,
just in case we forgot.

You were golden stardust awakening us
to the pink, cotton-candy sky—

the celebration of life as we knew it,
all rapturous and *full of glory!*

SECTION TWO

THE COCOON

Thunder grumbles, as the rain
lightly pitter-patters, like little
feet running. My cousin at age three

was jumping up to go to birthday
parties, grinning like a *Daschund*
puppy, happily bouncing on

his father's knee. He was a *spitting
image* of him, eating grape jam
out at grandma's house, and sitting at

her kitchen table next to me, facing
the window, where the miniature
sunlight became a floodlight of

stars, circling like doves, as we spent
time together on a Saturday
morning, waiting for the world

to spin us to another planet, or
to go on the hospital boat,
or back in time to the World's Fair, or to

FAO Schwartz, or to the plane-
tarium, or to *heaven* and back again.
Those few hours together were

like a lifetime of memories,
bound by a kitchen frame, like
we were the last people on the planet.

How I don't want that memory to fade—
to be discarded away,
like we were never idealistic

Christmas presents to our parents,
still lovely in their velvet skins,
and their hearts all a-glitter, like

butterflies breaking out of their cocoons.

ELEGY FOR COUSIN CHARLES

You suffocated from callous hands,
loss of love and desperate to make yourself

unborn again, graceful and free—
trying to reach beyond the stars to get

that tough love,
flying in the wind, bursting onto

my neighbor's brown lawn.
1000's of hugs, waste onto the trees

occluding your chance to breathe—
red, raw and itchy, bristling along

my legs spine.
You smelled like summer after it rained.

Have you ever redeemed yourself
from a life sentence?

"You can pretend to be the breeze
lifting you off to heaven,"

said a familiar voice so sweetly.
Babies are not chattel for lost love—

they are *angels.*
I hear the sounds of horns

and lutes in a symphony
under the eye of the killer loose inside us all—

that's where the *novacaine* must be fermenting.
And the rhythmic strumming of my fingers gets me high.

They have miniature love letters glued to their arches.

CHRISTMAS

It's Christmas week. Kyla your second cousin
has finished playing with all her new toys.

They lay spread out on the soft purple mat.
We have abandoned them after hours of fun

tracking light from them, then squeezing
the textures of sensory balls before playing

the drums & piano. It has been a joy;
I am exhausted. I dump the toys in

a box packed by the television. Next,
I leave to tuck Kyla into her electric

bed that she loves to go up & down on,
like a cool ride at the amusement park.

Just this fun feeling of moving is a thrill
for Kyla, as she giggles & smiles this huge

grin that infects you with all kinds of desires
for miracles, of *what if's* & *what will be's.*

I leave her bedroom to explore the living room
again. That's when the music starts to play

from one of her toys. I try to ignore it
thinking it has a faulty wiring or something,

but then it plays again as the other toys
start to play. I get this eerie feeling that

you are in the room playing with Kyla's toys.
You are smiling & looking at

me with those brown eyes that makes you
smile. I know you want to cry too, but you don't.

I want to reach out to you. I don't.
I just watch you. I wonder why you came back

to visit? Because it's Christmas?
So, we're all supposed to be happy?

How can there be so much happiness?
I almost don't want to believe that. Happiness

is transient. Sometimes we are dead to our emotions
and feel numb, like we are suffocating ourselves

with grief—we don't feel the air on our fingers.
We don't feel there is any oxygen. Our own

unhappiness has built a semi-private prison in which
we are to contain ourselves. The cold air can be

invigorating at times. Maybe it keeps us going?
When cool air tempers our bad nerves,

it acts as our clock in which we measure
how much we can handle. Will we leave

when it gets too unbearable, or will we
just sit it out, being strong & thankful

that we made it through one more Christmas
knowing we are not alone? We still have air—

we still have our memories; we still have
our senses shielding us from the hereafter.

DETAILS

Did she lay you down, in the bed, in the spot
your father would fall asleep on when next to her—

on top of the white embroidered bedspread—
your head slanted against a red satin pillow?

Or did she reach down into your toy-filled crib, then
drown the moist whispers of your warm, sweet dream

like a planet expunging its race to space?
Did she tell you before you were no longer

able to *breathe fire*, into the empty
cold apartment, that you were going to meet

sweet Jesus?—that you were a sacrifice for
her *tiny* God? Did she whisper lullabies

in your ear? Did she tell you, "I love you—but
I'm so *sorry*; I'm so *sorry*; I'm so *sorry*...?"

THE WAKE

When you died, they put you in
the same casket with your mother
nestled together. A red velvet
curtain wrapped around, like a
halo. I hated that image
years later. I didn't know who
it benefited, your mother
or you. Would you have had no
anger, if you had known? Would
you have wanted her love or
been forgiving & kind? And I
guess you would have been an
angel. Why had I
thought otherwise? I don't know—
I guess it's *heathenistic* nature
to imagine otherwise.
A sane person could only provide
a healing to one that had gone insane.

THE BLACK HOLE

The space is all black. The computer screen
exhales like rich black eyes oozing in onyx.

This is beauty nobody can enjoy.
It is the aftermath from years of absence

of not knowing you ever existed—
or asking, *why not?* It's wondering, *why*

your life was taken? How could it have been
prevented? Would you have survived otherwise

without your mother?—or if she were to
have been institutionalized? Would you

have been like Malcolm X?—or an orphan, or—
adopted? Would you have survived a stepmother?

Your dad remarried. Did you
ask yourself why she didn't just kill your dad?—

and not you. You were your own person—not
your dad, not your mom, just you. What could have

been was not; she *stole* your life and trashed her
own afterward. But I still ask, *what could*

have been? Maybe you could have been saved!—
had there been drugs for depression that worked—

had there been no *stigma*—
had your father loved her…

SLEEP

So sweet is the sound of heaven's lips purring.
The heart of hope, happy like a newborn and well rested.

The recuperating child's breaths, like snowflakes falling at
midnight—the lung's rise and exhalation, like a new car engine.

The ahhhhhh… of the heater next to you, like God painting
The Sistine Chapel, all in one day.

The hiss of your sighs and dreams
undoing all the charlatans, the snake charmers, the forgers—

the imposters—*those who say they don't love you!*
The plane is on autopilot, and I am the captain navigating

the turbulence, removing the murderers from their posts—
extinguishing them like flies populating the flower fields

of dreaming zinnias, forget me not's, sunflower's whirling in a joyful
dance—the dance of the courageous—the dance of the tigers and leopards—

the dance of the beasts—the lions and bears and bobcats.
The end of eternity plays its music in your ears, sweet, soft music:

The whispers of a blind snake praying in Portuguese…
Your pet dog walking past death's jaw.

The humming of your soul reincarnating.

TRAGEDY

Tragedy is our signature.
It sits on our tombstone.
It waits until snowfall.
It hides in our bones.
It fly's as an insect with larvae.
It can be contained.
It can be *eradicated* as weeds
pulled from the flower garden
until it blooms no more!

GOODBYE COUSIN CHARLES AND AUNTIE BETTY

Goodbye, I hope you know,
      I've missed you both.
Till we meet again.
      Adieu.

I've missed you both.
      Time escaped the black clouds.
Till we meet again.
      Au revoir.

Time escaped the black clouds.
      Black birds send love.
Till we meet again.
      Tchau.

Lisa Rhodes-Ryabchich is the proud single-mother of a special needs teenager and lives in Piermont, N.Y. She teaches poetry and screenwriting at Westchester Community College and has also taught a memoir, fiction, poetry writing class at Piermont Library and elsewhere. She performs her poetry throughout the United States and has two poetry chapbooks: *We Are Beautiful Like Snowflakes* (2016) and *Opening the Black Ovule Gate* (2018) both published with http://www.finishinglinepress.com Recently her first full-length poetry manuscript *Peripeteia* was published by Cyberwit.net and in 2021 another full-length poetry collection was published entitled *How You Get to There*. Her poetry blog and performance schedule is: http://www. lisarhodesryabchichpoetryblog.wordpress.com. She has a MFA in Poetry from Sarah Lawrence College, a B.A. in Communications from St. Thomas Aquinas College in Sparkill, N.Y., a Computer Science Certificate in Business Applications from SUNY Purchase in Purchase, N.Y., a B.S. in Journalism from Mercy College in Dobbs Ferry, N.Y., a Television News Production Certificate from New York University in Manhattan, N.Y., and a B.A. in Speech Pathology and Audiology from Lehman College in the Bronx, N.Y. She was a recipient of a 2016 scholarship with Martha's Vineyard Institute of Creative Writing. She is a reader for Empire Great Jones Little Press.

Furthermore, Lisa was a mentor for Pen America's Prison Writing Program, which helped prisoners reach their potential, promoted healing and rehabilitation.

Finally, her short story "Retribution On Cash Street" was published by Notyourmothersbreastmilk.com and her poems have been published or forthcoming in *Phantom Drift, Artemis Journal, Dash Literary Journal, Chaffey Review, Prachya Review, Nothing Substantial, The Writers Cafe Magazine, Madness Muse Press, Destigmatized: Voices for Change Anthology, 2019 Wordfest Anthology, Medical Literary Messenger,* http://www.moonmagazine. org., http://www.praxismagonline.com, *Gather Round: A Collaboration of Cave Canem Workshop and Retreat Poets, Obsidian III, Journal of Poetry Therapy, Footsteps, AIM, Left Jab, Poetry Motel,* poemhunter.com, *Peaceful Poetry to Love Your Societal Consciousness, Ancient Pathways,* and elsewhere. Her first

YA manuscript "You Don't Have to Tell Me I'm Innocent" was recently finished.

Her published articles are:

1.   Rhodes, L. (2011). Poetry writing as a healing method in coping with a special needs child: A narrative perspective. *Journal of Poetry Therapy: The Interdisciplinary Journal of Practice, Theory, Research and Education, V 24, n 2p.117-125 Sum*

2.   Rhodes, L. (2002). Poetry and a prison writing program: A mentor's narrative report. *Journal of Poetry Therapy, v15 n3 p163-68 Spr*

www.ingramcontent.com/pod-product-compliance
Lightning Source LLC
Chambersburg PA
CBHW021200090426
42740CB00008B/1169